RAINDROPS OF LOVE AND PAIN

THE AUTHOR DESCRIBES THE TRAUMA, HEARTBREAKS, BETRAYALS, LOVE, JOY, LIFE LESSONS SHE HAS EXPERIENCED THROUGH PROSE AND POETRY.

TASNEEM

To my mother, for everything you did for me. I owe you my life.

To my family and friends, who always encouraged me to do better.

To my babe, my better half, you mean the whole world to me.

To you, my dear reader, for purchasing my little piece of art.

Contents

Contents

Contents

Preface

Well, I always loved reading books, poetries, and hearing stories from my grandma. But I never wrote anything of my own. Until I fell in love and was betrayed, heartbroken, crushed. I started to write down whatever I felt in my diary. This book consists of all the things I've experienced, felt, and everything in between. It is said that love makes you a whole different person. I guess that's true because never in my wildest dreams I had thought I would write my very own book.

Acknowledgements

Firstly, Thank you God, for everything I have in my life.

I'd like to thank all my teachers from school to college, because of which I am able to read write and understand. Especially Rita Mam, our psychology teacher. She is a game changer for me.

Thank you my dear Maasi, I don't know what would I do without you.

I'd also like to thank my closest friends, especially Simran, Karishma, for always being by my side and encouraging me to do the best.

Many thanks to Mufaddal, your writings are superb, and you inspired me to be a writer as well.

Thank you to Notion Press and team, for giving budding authors like me a platform to show our writings to the world.

Lastly Thank you, to you, my dearest reader, who's holding a fragment of my heart right now in their hands, Thank you for reading this, I hope you'll treasure these words in your life forever. You hold a special place in my heart.

Koi agar mujhse ye puche, ke mein apni Maa ko kya kehta,

Na hota kufr duniya me, toh me apni Maa ko Khuda kehta.

-Amitabh Bachchan

Accha khaasa baithe baithe goom ho jaata hoon,

Ab mein aksar mein nahi rehta, tum ho jaata hoon.

-Anwar Shuoor

1. Love

About you.

Your eyes.

Your smile.

Your voice.

Your laugh.

Your lips.

Your kiss.

Your presence.

Your absence.

Everything about you feels different.

Flowers

Flowers grew wherever he touched me..

As we watch.

As we watch the beautiful sunset together, I realize that I want to be with you forever.

On a beach, with the faint sounds of waves, soothing and relaxing our craves.

You put your arms around my waist,

Tug me closer & our fingers interlaced.

As we watch the beautiful sunset, you realize that I'm your Juliet.

As we watch the sun slowly fade,

We realize how strong bond we've made.

You pull me closer to your body, then slowly lift up my chin,

Your eyes looking deeply in mine,

My goodness, even in darkness,

I could your eyes shine.

Then you put your arm around my waistline,

You slowly lean in, and your lips meet mine.

My God your lips tasted like wine,

And I was intoxicated.

We slowly pull away, and face towards the twilight sky, realizing,

Even Endings can be beautiful.

I woke up

I woke up wanting your lips on mine,

I woke up wanting your arms around my waistline,

I woke up wanting our hands interlaced,

I woke up wanting to look at your gorgeous face,

Most of all, I woke up, wanting you.

Love is everywhere.

I used to think that love was holding hands, kissing, cuddling, & promises.

Only after that you came then left, I realized that love is also my mother's-

"Why haven't you reached home yet?" and my friend's-

"Text me when you reach home."

Love is also the affection I feel towards the animals, the nature, food, books, libraries, places and my home.

Initially, I used to think love only exists between a husband and wife. That's not always true, though.

Sometimes love can exist everywhere but in a marriage. And sometimes love just exists everywhere.

We just need to change the way we look. Because some of the truest loves are **platonic.**

Pyaar.

Oh babe when I fell in love with you I fell in love with every crack in your skin, and every specks of light in your hazel brown eyes. I fell in love with the way you look while doing just normal things like riding a bike, writing in a book, or just simply walking. I fell in love with the way your eyes light up when you laugh. I fell in love with all of your happiness, sadness, madness, sorrow, everything.

Because when I said I love you, I fell in love with every bit of your body and soul.

- Shayad isse hi pyaar kehte hai.

2. Broken

Hopeless

I really hope you could see,

How precious you were to me...

- unrealistic hopes.

Do I ?

Many days later,

The tears still fall,

Why does it seem that I don't matter,

NO, not at all?

Your figure

I am here, standing in the pouring rain, to the faint outline of your figure. And as I go near, I see it disfigure.

Darling I want your arms around me, your lips on mine, kissing me slowly, with the faint sound of bonfire behind me.

You're always on my mind, wherever I go,

I see your figure in the storm,

and in the rain,

and in the snow.

But as I go near, I see it disappear.

Hence, I start to leave, and oh! I see you again.

But now I know that I'm insane.

And sadness is all that'll remain.

Distanced?

Two people,

Tied by a bond,

On one bed.

Together yet miles apart.

Ugh

Loving you unconditionally gave me nothing.

Except pain, tears, and regret.

Its hard.

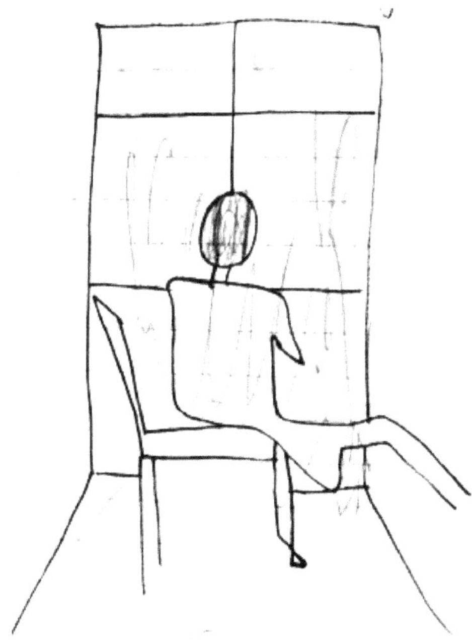

Oh darling, accept the fact that he never loved you..

Trapped

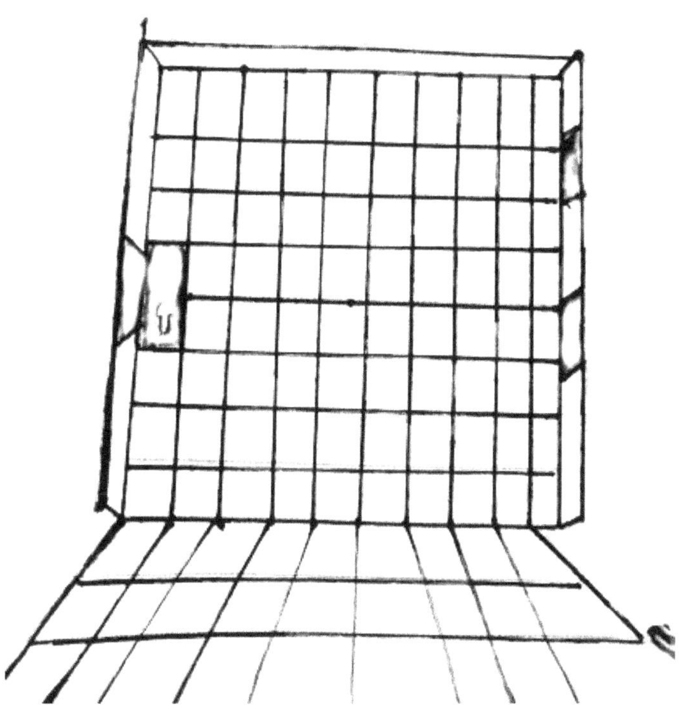

Every living being on this earth is free.

Except humans.

Humans are prisoners to time & society.

Betrayal

Getting betrayed by the person

I loved the most

I trusted the most

I looked up to the most,

Was, is, and will always be

the most heartbreaking

the most heart wrenching, &

the most depressing thing in my life.

Nightmare pt1

Falling in love with you was my sweetest dream,

whereas

You never falling for me,

was my worst nightmare.

Kiss

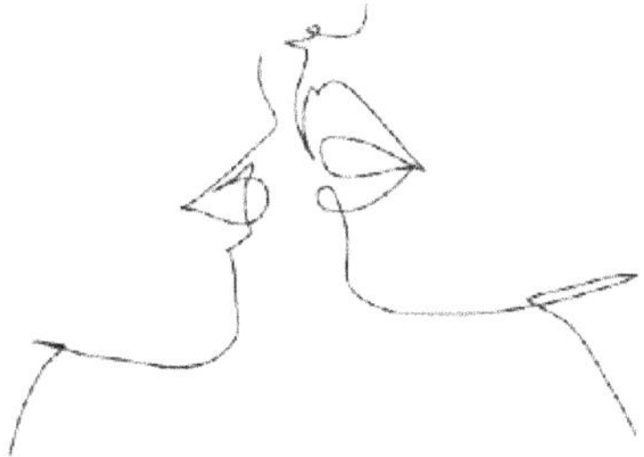

I'd touch you but the world wouldn't be the same again.

I'd hold you in my arms and never let you go

even in the rain

even in the snow.

I'd love you forever darling but I'm afraid that

I'll kiss you and lose you all over again.

Drowning

You took the life out of me and pretended you were breathless.

You saw that I was drowning, but you didn't care nevertheless.

You knew what was coming, you saw it with your own eyes,

But you still pretended you saw nothing and I believed all your lies.

-You knew it would hurt.

Just for the sake

'We seem distant lately,' he said.

'Were we even close enough to be distant?'. She replied.

-Majbooriyan.

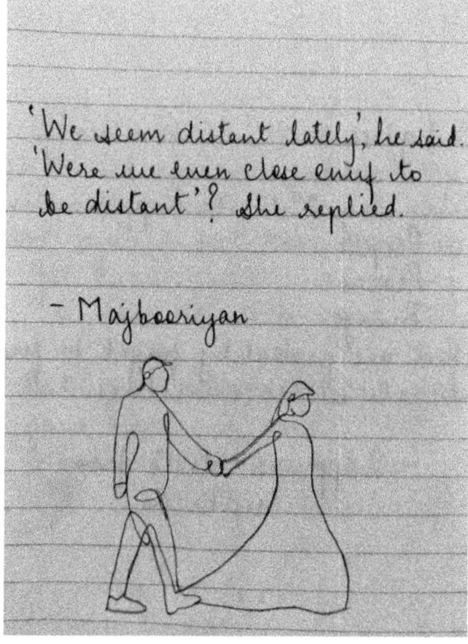

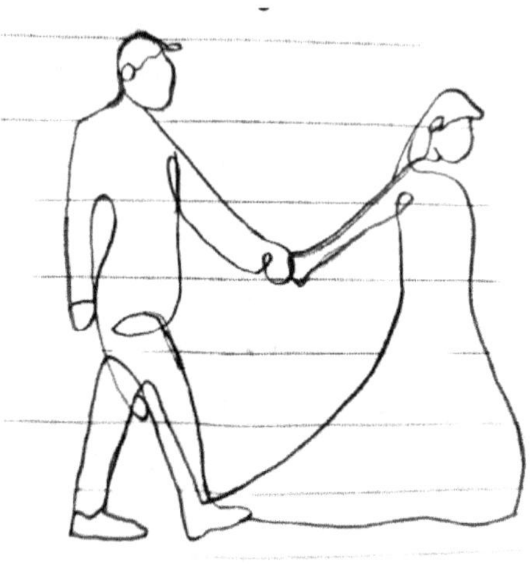

Lol I just clicked the photo from my phone and removed its background. But the lines stayed.

Just for the sake pt2

"I'm sorry." She said.

'Why?'. He asked, puzzled.

"I wasn't good enough for you to fall in love with me." She replied

Deceiver.

"I love you," he said.

"I'll love you forever and ever. Till death do us part."

As he said those words, his gaze pierced right through my heart.

He used to tell me everything me everything.

He loved me

Understood me

Took care of me on the days I felt low

He helped me grow.

I thought I was very special to him,

Very special,

Very important,

Very precious.

Until that day,

When I saw him with her,

She touching her face softly

He kissing her fondly.

I sighed

I cried

I died from inside.

The next morning he came to my home,

I opened tbe door, and shouted "Please leave!"

He smiled calmly and said, "Yes I'll leave but I wanna tell you
something first,"

He leaned closer to me, and whispered in my ear, "I love you, till
death do us part."

He leaned even closer, hugged me, and his hand slowly reached to
his pocket,

He took out a knife,

Stabbed her in the back

He killed his wife.

He ended her life.

The things you did

You abused me

bruised me,

accused me,

Later u took advantage of and used me.

You replaced me,

Disgraced me

Defaced me

Erased me

Some days these thoughts still break me........

You said you'd hold me and love me even if its cold.

You told me our love is precious just like gold.

Darling you were so good before so now what happened?

You were so sure of not to have your spirits dampened.

But I guess I was wrong,

I thought your love was strong,

I thought we could stand every storm,

I thought us to last long.

I ran through the crowds,

The sun finally appeared after all those grey clouds,

The sun shone bright

You were out of sight

My lips defined into a smile

I was the Lily of the Nile.

Yes, you were my sunshine, but you soon became my rain.

You tossed me

Exhausted me,

But that's okay, cuz I no longer feel the pain.

Cuz, now you lost me and I endure again.

Nightmare pt 2

I always had nightmares of us breaking apart,

And now that we are apart,

Perhaps its my nightmare but your dream...

- Because you never loved me.

Alone

She was sitting on the green grass next to her car,

And spotted a shooting star.

She wished her memories to blur,

While she played "their" favourite song on her guitar.

- One last time.

Burn

Burn down the memories,

Before they burn you.

- Erase it all. Don't hurt yourself.

IDK

"Just keep going"

- What if I can't?

Amidst the chaos.

In the midst of trying to constantly fit in,

I lost my true self.

Your text

You said you'd text me back,

You said you'd call me back,

and I kept waiting n waiting..

But your text never came

your call never came..

I guess you never felt shame!

& now I burn inside like a flame!

So this what I get for loving you?

Oh now my days are blue,

The night seems endless

but I still look for you

I still look for a clue.

I look here and there

and everywhere.

but I am lost.

The windows are covered in frost.

Darling now you look for me

but baby I am gone.

You search for me but I am gone.

And then you regret

You try to forget

But you can't.

And all you can do is remember..

Remember our mornings

cuddled up in bed

Remember our late night binge watches

cuddled up in bed.

Your thoughts are filled with me..

Tears rolling down your cheeks.

But babe, I am gone,

And now I feel strong

And I wish you live long

so that you could see me succeed without you all along..

And now I feel so delighted about the fact that you never texted me back!!

Chain

I love you but you love someone else, and that someone else loves someone else.

and this vicious cycle keeps on going.

Fake love

There's no such thing as true love in today's generation.

Its all just infatuation .

Oh no

Would you still love me even after knowing all my flaws? Even after knowing everything I've done in the past?

- I hope you say 'yes'.

People.

There's a certain element of truth

behind everything a person does.

Everything that people do,

tells you a little something about them.

Insecurities.

Why do I hate myself so much? Everytime I try to compliment myself my stupid brain turns it around on me and I end up feeling worse. Everytime I try to be affirmative, my mind immediately drifts off to my cellulite, body fat, skin color, my acne, how I mess up things everytime and I've never made anyone proud of having me. Then I cry. Why am I like this? **Why I can't be <u>like her?</u>** She has perfect skin. Perfect body. Beautiful face. She's so full of talent and creativity. She has a perfect family. Everyone loves her. Everyone likes to be around her. While here I am, nobody likes to be near me or be my friend. The people I have in my life as friends, I know they are fake. **She's everything that I've always wished for. She's everything that I can never be.**

From my desk.

Here I am, sitting at my desk, with my laptop on, looking for words to write.

Sometimes an energy flows through me and I can't stop writing. While on other days I can't think of anything at all no matter how hard I try. On some days I want to share my musings with the world. While on some days I just want to keep it to myself. And on some days, I just want to share it with you. In the hope of that maybe, just maybe, you'll fall in love with the words and eventually fall in love with the person who wrote them. Like how it happens in the movies. But I forget that this isn't a work of fiction. Things are different here. We can't dream of having a happily ever after in this world. It only exists in the fictional world. And so here I am, sitting at my desk, as I write these words, hoping it'll reach you someday.

- I wish this reaches you.

The hurting.

You know babe? It hurts. Its actually frrreaakinnggg hurts.

When someone means everything to you. But you mean nothing to them. I understand that you don't love me, and I am not forcing you to love me as well. I am just asking you to respect and reciprocate the feeling. Just call me once in a day, hell, even once in a week would do. Talk to me about your feelings. Your likes. Your dislikes. Try to understand me and my feelings. My past. Go on dates with me. Love will happen. Not immediately but gradually, yes. Love will happen only if u try. If u keep thinking about your ex and ways to get back, love will never blossom in this relationship. With us. Neither of us will be happy and contented with each other. You need to make time for love, for love to happen.

Will you?

If you're going to fall in love with me, please note that, loving me won't be easy.

I cry often, whether its during a movie, web series, a sad song on spotify, or just a nostalgic sunday evening.

I'll cry even when I'll be speaking of stuff that have hurt me in the past, even though they don't hurt me anymore. I am afraid of being alone, being left out, I'm afraid of failing, I am afraid that I am not good enough, I am afraid of the dark. Most of the time I am insecure about myself, you'll find me telling you things about myself that I hate. And even though you try to disagree I'll still be adamant. No matter how many times you tell me that you love me I'll still be afraid of losing you. Its not that I doubt your love, its that I doubt myself. I don't blame you though, for anything. I feel empathy for every being surrounding me. Most of the times, I am a mess. SO tell me my dear, will you still love me after knowing about all of my doubts, trauma, insecurities, and the things that have happened to me in the past?

A place in my heart.

There's a corner in my heart that is yours. And I don't mean for now, or until I've found someone else, I mean forever. I mean to say that whether I fall in love a thousand times or never again, there'll always be a small teeny tiny place reserved for you in my soul. ALWAYS. What I've felt for you, I'll never feel for anybody else.

I want fresh air.

I find myself lacking, as if I should be complete. Someone is whispering to me that this life doesn't belong to me. Its like I have another life left in half. I'm always pressurized by the people surrounding me to constantly look perfect and be an ideal woman and make them proud. I feel like escaping, to somewhere far away, leaving all this mess behind me and never to think about it. To start anew. I wish I could escape from this reality that tries to mould me into something I am not, that tries to cage my soul into their rusty, old, orthodox prison.

- Its suffocating, I want to breathe.

A decoy.

The way he smiled at her, the way he made her feel complete, the way he looked at her, it was all a lie, a decoy, to conceal his real self. He just wanted the throne, nothing else. He broke her and she would never be the same again.

Empty

This feeling of emptiness, doesn't leave me.

It always overpowers, and rules.

Its like I am whole, but empty.

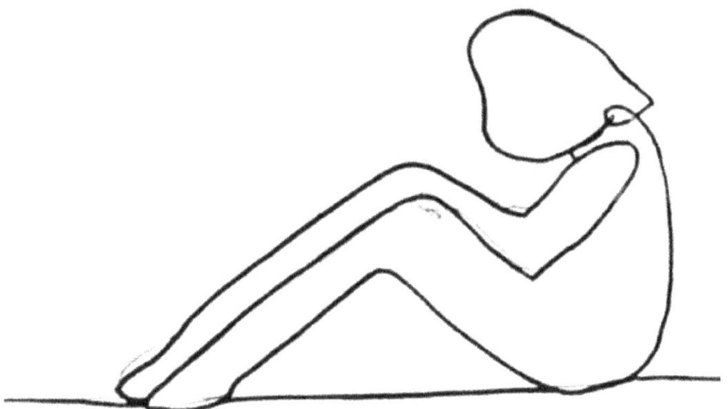

Lets meet soon.

The feeling of your hand in mine, our fingers interlaced, your smile, your laugh, your voice, our kiss, are the only things that prevents me from losing my sanity. The days we spent together, our late night video calls, our moments of joy and tears, all these are still fresh in my heart. Like it just happened yesterday.

Sometimes, I wake up in the middle of the night hoping to find you by my side. Next to my pillow. I feel empty not seeing you there.

Do you still remember me? Am I still on your mind?

"As long as one is alive in your mind and you in them, distance wouldn't matter." I had read this somewhere. These words keep me alive and hopeful.

Its been a long time since we last met, but I still hope to stay in your mind just like you in me.

what I deserve?

Why is it that whenever I feel genuinely happy from inside, from
within,

Life happens, and it pulls me down so badly,

As if I don't deserve to be happy,

As if I don't deserve happiness at all.

As if I don't deserve joy,

<u>As if I am only meant to deserve sorrow.</u>

YOUR FIGURE

Here I am, standing in the pouring rain, to the faint outline of

your figure,

And as I go near,

I see it disfigure...

Darling, I want your arms around me, your lips on mine, kissing

me slowly,

With faint sound of the waves, behind me.

You're always on my mind, wherever I go,

I see your figure in the storm and

In the rain, and

In the snow.

But as I go near, I see it disappear.

Hence, I start to leave,

And OH!! I see you again,

But now I know that I am insane

I feel the pain

And sadness is all that'll remain.

Arranged? Forced?

Two people,

Tied by a bond,

On one bed.

Together yet miles apart.

Pain.

Loving you unconditionally, gave me nothing.

Except pain, tears and regret.

A delusion

OHH Darling, please,

Accept the fact that he never loved you...

- get out of this illusion

3. SELF HARM

Inducing self harm doesn't make you strong, and it doesn't make you weak either.
It leaves you in between, nowhere, as if you're taking a road that has no destination.

CUTS

Whenever I think of doing it,

I tell myself that I'm strong, I wouldn't do such things.

But then why is it that when I align the blad across my wrist, I start shivering and then put it away?

Am I really strong or

Am I actually afraid and weak?

- thoughts before self harm.

UGLY.

They called me fat

They called me ugly,

So I decided to cut down

to slit down my fat.

Now my scars are ugly.

-whatever I do, they don't seem to like it.

Numb

I need to feel something even if its pain.

even if its a blade running across my vein...

CANVAS.

Her brush was the knife,

Her canvas, her body.

And she carved wonderful illustrations.

If you looked closely, each carving had a story to tell.

NUMB THE PAIN

Everyone has their own way of numbing out the pain,

For some its clubs, drinking, dancing,

While some prefer cigarette, hookah and cocaine,

While mine happens to be running a blade across my vein..

4. SOME GOOD STUFF? MAYBE.

THE MOVIE

I read somewhere, idk where, 'to live for the little things in life.'

Live for the 5AM sunrises, and the 7PM sunsets.

Live for the rain. For the sun. For the moon.

For the summer. For the winter.

Live for the rainbows in the sky, the colors that we don't usually see.

Also live for the thunderstorms and the grey skies.

Live for the road trips, the train journeys, the bike rides, the flights, the layovers, and everything in-between.

Live around the people who make you realize that the world isn't a bad place afterall.

This is what life is all about. The little things that makes up a whole huge movie, called 'LIFE'.

And you my dear reader, are the director, producer, writer, of this movie.

Phases of the moon.

Some days I feel weak, some days I feel tired, some days I look at the words that I've written and feel good, but I don't feel their passion or bravery. I have a bad tendency of talking only about the days where I feel sad, grey and empty. I don't talk about the days where I feel good, better, and productive. Those days are there though. Those days do happen yes not very often, but they are there. I'm scared that if I talk about those days, I'll jinx it and catch an evil eye. There's nothing to worry about me though. I am fine. I change. Like the moon. I am like the moon. Like how moon has its phases, I do too. Sometimes I am all dark, and invisible. Sometimes I am all bright, like a new moon.

Freedom of words.

sometimes I feel like a writer. Not like any old writer, but like myself. I have so much to say. But most of the time it gets caught in my throat and I choke on my own words and thoughts. It's like my thoughts are overflowing out of my mind and are searching for a pen and paper to settle themselves. As I hurriedly search for a medium to write those words down, a thought crosses my mind. If I write them down, I'll put them in a cage from where they can never be free. Yes, they'll be protected, but I'll take away their freedom.

Hence, I stop searching for the pen and paper, and allow my words to flow away freely. If they're meant to be mine, they'll come to me again someday. And then I'll set them free by writing it down in my diary and sharing it them with the world.

- Whatever I share with the world, goes through a lot of filtration process in my mind.

My escape.

I long to balance my practicality with my dreaming. I try to built a narrative that shifts from my present to my potential. People call it daydreaming. NO. **I CALL IT MY ESCAPE.** My escape from reality. My escape from everything. My dreams that can't be a reality. Perfect body. Perfect skin. Perfect marriage. These things helps me in being sane. That one day, maybe one day, just one day, all that I've ever dreamed of, will come true.

I live for that one day. It keeps me alive.

WHAT IS LOVE?

Have you ever heard the word 'LOVE?' No, I don't mean through those whatsapp messages, or insta DM's. Not the the chemical reaction love that science says. Not the movie dialgoues.

I mean looking into someone's eyes under the stars, while they tuck your hair behind your ear.

I mean late at night while walking home after dinner.

I mean writing letters, or making personal notes about each other everyday because you miss them and can't wait to see them again.

I mean, hearing someone mean the word 'LOVE'.

Because I know, I haven't.

A void in her heart.

She put her hand on her chest. She said, 'look, look right here.' She guided his hand towards her heart.

'Something seems to be missing inside my heart. It's kinda lacking something. It feels empty. No matter whatever I do, that void doesn't fill, doesn't diminish, doesn't vanish."

The right person at the wrong time.

"You loved her didn't you?" she said softly, looking into her eyes.

He stood there with his unwavering gaze, knowing that she's right.

"I did, but that doesn't mean I can't love you."

"You're right, you can love me but,.. but you'll never love me as much as you loved her. I saw the way you looked at her, her eyes were the only ones you'd search for in a crowded room. She.. she... is perfect according to you. I understand why you picked her, but my eyes will never be her eyes, mine will never make your heart race, mine will never make you feel like nothing else matters in this world."

He looked away with guilt written all over his face.

She took a deep breath and said, " You could atleast look at me."

Their eyes met.

"I never meant to hurt you."

"I know," she said, brushing off a tear from his beautiful face. A face that meant everything to her. A face that was her safe haven.

A heaven.

"It won't hurt anymore now." She whispered.

He nodded, knowing she deserved so much more. She nodded too, knowing that he deserved more.

They both looked at each other and smiled, one last time.

Within

I guess this is where we go wrong,

We try to locate happiness in

people

places

things.

But we probably forget to first locate it in ourselves.

- happiness starts from with 'in'

SELF LOVE

I was waiting for someone

to love me

to hold me

to protect me

To love me when I'm low and

To love me when I'm high.

But I never found any such someone though.

Later I found myself the love for which I was always waiting

when I started loving myself without hesitating.

Because 'I LOVE MYSELF' is the

quietest

simplest

most powerful revolution ever.

5. RANDOM POV's

A collection of random POV's that came across my mind either while listening to a certain type of song, melody, or while watching a movie, or simply while just walking down the street. I mean.. I can include this section right? Is it acceptable? I hope you don't mind.

BETRAYAL

SYNOPSIS- You are the queen of your country. But you don't seem happy in your marriage.

****

And now, I pronounce you as the queen and king of the royal country!"

I still have the moment in front of my eyes. The day you betrayed me. You told me you don't want the royal crown.

But here we are – sitting on the throne, solving the dumb issues. Didyou ever love me?Did you ever care for me? I know the answer. And it's quite heart wrenching.

And you know what?

I completely get it. I know it's my fault. I thought that your love for me was genuine. But no, I was so wrong.

"How's the food, my love?" I ask in a soft voice. You don't even look at me, shrugging your shoulders, and nodding slightly.

The night progresses, the banquet gets more cheerful. Until you collapse.

"Someone, call the royal doctor! Hurry! The king isn't breathing!"

I fell on the floor, crying. But underneath, I am smiling.

My main maid comes over, whispering to me: "It is your time, my queen."

You died of natural causes. No one noticed the poison in your drink that I made. My maids got rid of it effectively.

The funeral was long and boring, mostly tiring. I had to fake crying so many times.

So I hope you are watching from Hell.

"And now, I pronounce you as the queen of this royal country!"

This country is mine now. As it should.

A ROMAN MYTHOLOGY

SYNOPSIS- The goddess of tranquility , Tranquillitas. It's her job to maintain calm & peace amongst the hearts of every human. On the other hand, she also happens to be your guardian angel. Right now you're in a complete mess.

THEME- ROMAN MYTHOLOGY, FICTION, DRAMA.

GENRE- SHORT STORY.

(A meeting between the Gods in heaven.)

"Goddess Tranquillitas, what's wrong with your child?" Jupiter; the king of Gods asked.

"Lord, she's unable to find calm and peace within herself. She's been highly influenced by her peer groups, social media, and her step-siblings. She's constantly under pressure to prove herself that she's better than everyone else." The Goddess replied.

"So how will you heal her?"

"I'll try my best. Grant me some time, my king."

"Take as much time as you want, but there should be remarkable results."

"I won't disappoint you, my Lord." The goddess stated, bowed down, and left.

(On Earth)

"Hey Jemima!! Pass me the ball!!" One of the players who also happened to be the college's badass bully, shouted at me at the basketball practice.

"If you pass her the ball, she'll take the winning goal, and it's your right since ur the closest to the basketball net. C'mon just ignore her and jump!!" (The Goddess told her.)

I don't know why, but somehow passing her the ball seemed wrong. As if my instincts were telling me to do something else. Nevertheless, I shook away the feeling and passed her the ball. She received it and made the goal. Later, the coach appreciated her skills. And I felt bad because it was me who had done the groundwork, but as always, I was never recognized.

If only I had listened to my gut feeling. I sighed to myself. Anyways, I was done for the day, hence I took my belongings and started to leave. There on the exit gate, there was a group of senior boys doing God knows what. But one person caught my eye. My childhood friend and crush, Jalen. Aka the college's Prince Charming. You'll find almost every girl simping over him. Especially that bully who previously took the credit. What's her name again? Ah yes, Vanessa. Duh. I simply kept looking at him from a distance, because if i would get noticed, I'd be damned.

"When are you gonna confess your feelings to him?" A voice told me from within.

Donno man. Not now. Maybe when I become successful and pretty like those other girls on social media. I gazed at myself. I was wearing a pink pullover with purple watercolour print, and skinny black jeans. My hair was as usual tied in a bun, (because i had very long hair, up till my waist, and people made fun of me, called me old fashioned if I left it open. And I never wanted to chop down my hair. I never liked to do any sort of modification to my hair. Like trimming, cutting, dying, highlighting, etc.) and I was wearing blue nikes. Basically I looked like a nerd. Well yeah my grades were pretty excellent and I was good in sports too, but in terms of fashion and social skills, I was a zero.

I felt bad about myself. And I just ran past them so that they couldn't notice me. But I did feel a pair of eyes watching me. I didn't pay much heed to it and quickly took my cycle and rode home.

******A few days later*******

My days were going pretty normal, I was now kinda accustomed to the shaming, whispering and the torture of my stepsisters at home. Sometimes I felt like leaving all of this mess and running far away from all this. But of course that would be very risky and a rash decision.

One day, the college announced a farewell party for the seniors. And it was our batch's responsibility to organize everything. We all were busy in the preparations. Then finally the day arrived. Everybody from our class and the seniors were present. Including him. He was dressed in formals, and was looking hella handsome. While I was dressed in a shimmering golden coloured silk gown, and high heels. My makeup was minimal. And I had changed my hairstyle from a bun to a french braid. I looked very simple and bland compared to the other girls in the party. I sat next to my bff Christie and we talked randomly. Until some noises caught my attention. I went towards the crowd to see what was happening and what I saw shattered my heart.

Jalen, the love of my life, was passionately kissing Vanessa!

I almost fell to the ground. My face felt hot and I felt tears strolling down my cheeks. I covered my face and immediately left from there. I came on to the terrace and sat in a corner. I put my head between my legs and cried miserably. There was no peace in my life. "They say there's a goddess of tranquility, who provides peace to the human heart. Where are you?! Why aren't you blessing me with peace?! WhY?? What have I done?!" I angrily looked up at the sky and shouted. But there was utter silence. I started crying again. A few moments later, I heard footsteps approaching me. I looked up and I didn't believe what I saw. I was probably hallucinating.

"Hey Jam! Why did you rush out of the party? ..Uh.. Omg are you crying? What happened?"

It was really him!! It was Jalen! He always used to call me Jam. I didn't understand what to do.. In order to not make things even worse.. I got up and decided to leave.

He held my wrist and pulled me towards him. I was now facing him and our faces were only inches apart. My heart was beating so fast I thought it'll just come out of my chest.

"Do you know that I hate it when I see you cry? So please tell me what happened?" His voice oozed with compassion and love.

I was melted at his gaze, and for once, I decided to trust my instincts and give it a shot.

"I-I- I already had a bad day and when I saw you kissing Vanessa, I, I, just-"

"Just what?" He said, suddenly grabbing my waist and pulling me closer to him.

"I don't know.. I felt. ..-"

"That it should be you kissing me instead?" He completed the sentence himself.

I stood there in silence. A cold breeze ran through the atmosphere and he took it as a yes, and leaned in and kissed me. We kissed for a long time.

"Jam, I have always admired you and liked you since school, but I was afraid to tell you what I feel, cuz I didn't wanna lose you. What happened down with Vanessa was nothing serious. She literally begged me to kiss her at the party. And in order to get rid of her, I said yes. That's it. I always had my eyes on you. I've never liked any other woman besides you."

"But what do you like about me? I'm not even that fashionable or something like that"

"I like you, for you. You are just perfect the way you are. You don't need to change anything at all. "

That night.. I realized that the only way one can truly find peace in themselves is when they accept who they are, just the way they are, and stop comparing themselves to others.

(In heaven)

"Great work Goddess! I'm impressed with your intellect ."
Exclaimed Lord Jupiter.

"Thank you Lord. Afterall, the Goddess of Wisdom happens to be
my sister." She stated sarcastically.

THE CHOSEN ONE

THEME- HARRY POTTER FICTION.

SYNOPSIS- You're Draco Malfoy and you've been chosen to kill Albus Dumbledore.

You will kill Albus Dumbledore, young Malfoy," the Dark Lord hissed. "Or I will kill you instead."

"Yes, my lord," I bowed down, completely oblivious to the fact that the Dark Lord had threatened to end the Malfoy line.

Hence i started to plan several things but all of them seemed to fail. Nothing seemed to work. I tried to poison his drink but Harry dropped it by mistake. All my attempts were failing.

A few days later, The dark lord called for a meeting.

" I had given you one job, Draco! And this is how you reward me?"

"Apologies, my lord. I am trying my best. But he is in full security. I can't do anything."

"Well then.. If you can't... then I will... Lucius...Please bring her..."

Moments later my father entered with a girl whose hands were tied with magic rope and her mouth was shut. I immediately recognized her.

"Astoria!! WHat is she doing here!!!!" I asked my father, rage dwelling up inside me.

"Well you see… We know the eternal bond you both share .. so my dear malfoy…this is your punishment…" The dark lord whispered and smirked evilly.

"W-hat w-hat what do you mean?? I'll do my job!! Just gimme some time!! Lord ple-"

Before I could complete my sentence… I saw a wand swinging up in the air and a blinding green light filled the room.

"Avada Kedavra."

The spell of death.

The killing curse.

Moments later, the light disappeared and my eyes adjusted to the darkness around me. But everything around me became blurred as I saw Astoria's body lying on the ground. I rushed towards her.

"Astoria !! Astoria!! Noooo!! Please wake up!!!.

But she didn't. She wouldn't listen to me. To my pleas. She was lying there on the ground. Cold. Lifeless. Dead.

She always hated the dark chill of the Manor, "Their hearts are desolate, please leave them." She always used to tell me. I wish I had listened to her. I wish I hadn't listened to my father. I wish I could do more for her. But now, here I am standing next to her cold lifeless body, remembering all those good times we had. I never knew what death felt like. I never knew how it feels when someone who means the whole world to you, dies in front of your eyes and you are unable to do anything. Just stand there like a dead corpse.

Her death made me realize something. Her death made me realize Harry's pain.

I wiped my tears, took her delicate body in my arms, and turned towards the dark lord.

"Thank You, Lord. I'll try my best to protect Hogwarts and their residents. Even at the cost of my life. Do whatever you want." I declared with utter confidence as I left the manor, with grief, with pride.

RUA

"The moon is beautiful, isn't it?" she said as she slowly turned her head.

it was nothing but silence as she looked at the grass.

a tear fell from her face.

"i wish you were still here to see it with me" she said smiling

she looked back up at the moon.

"Yeah, I wish you were here."

POV: tonight's a full moon and you want to write something poetic. But your head hurts so much and you had a difficult month. Your eyes are sore and itchy from weeping over the loss of him. Thus, you simply lay down and relax on the floor, while the moonlight fills in your room. Dreaming of touching the moon and the Heavens someday, you play this tune on your piano.

"Hey, let's dance under the moonlight, shall we?" You heard a voice while you were playing the piano.

You get startled, and turn around to see, but there's no one.

"Yeah, sure." You said loudly.

You dance in the moon-lit room alone in your silk pink gown.

You move and groove in such a way that a spectator would think you're a trained ballerina.

"People think I'm crazy. That I keep imagining you even though you're not here." You whisper while he slowly slides his arms on your waist.

"Let them think. They're wrong anyways. You know that I'm here, that's all that matters. He smiled while looking into my eyes.

"Rua." I whispered his name.

"Hmmm..?" He replied while leaning in.

You kept playing the piano music under the sparkling moonlight and with each spin, you kept glancing at him. Rua. Your moon.

How beautiful he looked.

You had no words to describe how you felt, feeling full and empty all at once.

P. S. - Rua means moon.

That Ferris Wheel

TOPIC- PICTURE PROMPT (FERRIS WHEEL)

SYNOPSIS- Draco Malfoy is your longtime crush. You deeply love him. On the day before Christmas, he escorts you towards the forest.

THEME- Harry Potter fiction.

"Where are we going? I think we aren't allowed to come here." I say anxiously.

"Ssshh, keep quiet and just follow me." He says looking straight ahead, while holding his wand tight in his left hand.

As we walked, I could sense someone following us. I kept looking behind to see who it was, but there was no one. A few moments later, I heard the snapping of a twig. Before I could turn around and see who it was, Draco immediately came front and took me in his arms, and without giving it a second thought he raised his wand in mid-air and shouted

"Sectumsempra!" (causes severe lacerations)

I heard a thud, someone fell on the ground.

"Are you okay?" he looked at me, with concerned eyes, and asked.

"UHmm yes yes. But who was he?"

"If my guess is correct, then, it was a Death Eater."

"Whattt????" I almost fell on the ground. His arms tightened around me.

"Oh chill, he's probably gone now. Let's proceed further." His demeanour was calm and collected, unlike mine, I was in utter panic and fear.

"Ah but why were they following us?" I asked in utter confusion. As far as I remember, death eaters hated muggles, and neither of us were muggles.

"They were here for me." he said, his voice was soft, his eyes seemed guilty.

"WHY?? What have you done?"

"I broke the most important rule."

"Which?" I was totally confused.

"Not to fall in love."

"HAHAHA, MALFOY!! R U KIDDING ME?? THE DRACO MALFOY, IS IN LOVE??!?!?!? I started laughing uncontrollably.

"Yes." He replied with such sincerity, all of my doubts immediately vanished. As if he casted some spell on me.

Before I could ask or say anything, he raised his wand in mid air and swirled it while saying "Parco divertimenti" (a charm that changes your surroundings into an amusement park.)

WOW. From a fearful deadly forest, my surroundings changed into a romantic amusement park, with lights, food stalls, ferris wheel, and everything that I loved.

Then Malfoy kneeled to the ground.

"Orchideous." (a charm that produces flowers.) He took those flowers in his hand, looked up at me and said," Ella, I love you. I have loved you for a long time, and now I can't hide it from you anymore. My heart aches when I see you talking to Harry, my heart aches when I realize the fact that I can't even look at you properly. Because of this dumb thing that I got chosen. I have left the death eaters, hence they are trying to kill me. But before I get killed, I want to tell you how I feel about you. Ella, I love you with all my heart."

I was dumbfounded. I didn't know what to do, what to say, how to react. I simply stood there, agape. Draco loved me back too!!

He slowly stood up and gently grabbed my face. HE slowly leaned in, and you two kissed.

Deep

Beautiful

Passionate.

Stars, fireworks, butterflies, I felt everything all at once.

FERRIS WHEEL

Author's Letter

Hii there my dear reader!

Let's be a little informal here, and have a one on one conversation, a sincere heart to heart talk.

You and me, were born on this earth, for a reason.

Our journey here, isn't an easy ride. It ain't a smooth road at all. It's all bumpy, cracky, and full of potholes (jaise mumbai ki sadke). Magar mumbai ki sadko ka bhi ek alag hi maza hai. If you don't know what a bad road feels like, you wouldn't realize the value of a good, clean and smooth road.

Life happens. Bad things happen. But good things happen too.

Bad things won't last, and similarly the good things won't last too.

The bad and the good road will keep on coming simultaenously.

While you're on your bad days, if you keep thinking about how bad they are, you'll miss the view.

On the bad roads, the car slows down a bit, right? And then you can have a good look at your surroundings, the hills, the rivers, the mountains. But if you do not look outside the window, because you're busy complaining about how bumpy and uncomfortable the ride is, you'll miss all the mesmerzing and breathtaking views that the nature is offering to you. You'll never come back to this road again, since its a one way. You won't be able to experience it again.

And then one day, you'll regret.

I've been through a lot in life, and I'm sure you've been through a lot too. But here we are, despite it all. What if you and I kept thinking about how bad the road is, and decided to stop the car, and not move at all? Would you and I be here? Would have I been able to write this book, and would you my dear reader be able to read this?

Remember, that no matter how hard life gets, do not harm yourself. Do not induce self harm. Its a blackhole. Once you step in there's no escape. And God forbid, if you're already in, please seek help. I do not encourage any one of you to induce injury upon yourselves. So please, keep going. I know it sounds very cliche but that's what you gotta do. All your life. Make good memories. Enjoy this lovely and adventurous journey called "LIFE".

These words, this letter, its not only for you. It's for me as well. On the days where I'll feel low, where I'll feel like giving up, I'll come back to this letter. It's a souvenir for me. And I hope it becomes yours too.

Lastly, I'd like to confess something to you my dear reader-
"I LOVE YOU."
Yours truly,
Tasneem.